Odyssey and Other Poems

2ND EDITION

JOSEPH F. GABRIEL

Outskirts Press, Inc.
http://www.outskirtspress.com

ISBN: 978-1-4787-8508-8

Outskirts Press and the "OP" logo are trademarks belonging to Outskirts Press, Inc.

PRINTED IN THE UNITED STATES OF AMERICA

For Eleanor Greiner Gabriel

And In Memory of

My Father, Joseph Gabriel, Sr.
My Mother, Almarinda Rossi Gabriel
And My Brother, Robert E. Gabriel

Acknowledgments

The following poems first appeared as indicated:

"Agent 007" in *Italian Americana*

"Bronstein" in The Hampden-Sydney Poetry Review

"Fairy Godfather" in The Hampden-Sydney Poetry Review:

"Grandmother's House" in *Italian Americana*

"Joey Jazz" on the *Italian Americana* website

""Odyssey" in *Italian Americana*

"Paul Arrives in Athens" in The Classical Outlook

"Prolegomenon to the Theoretic of Randomness and Whim" in The Hampden Sydney-Poetry Review

"Remembering Ingrid" in *Italian Americana*

"Story Time" in The Hampden-Sydney Poetry Review

"Two-Ton Tony" in *Italian Americana*

An earlier version of "Days of Junior High and War" called "School" appeared in Imagi

"Lamplighter" in Gradiva

Contents

Jottings

Poetry

The saint damns poetry as "Devil's wine,"
Still, I drink—transgression, lovely, mine.

Piety

My thanks to God for gravity
A gift of His forethought and grace
Without it, surely, I'd be lost
Adrift, alone, in endless space

Miss Mafia Muffet

Miss Mafia Muffet
Annoyed to find
Another upon her tuffet
With mayhem in mind
Summoned her hitman inclined
The usurper to terminally buffet

Not Redon's Bouquet

Do you remember

Your farewell, one day,

The gift you gave me,

Was not Redon's bouquet

But another green vase

You found in love's maze

That somehow contained

Those uprooted red roses

Your farewell ordained,

All unaware,

In their goodbye poses,

Of their own despair

Pen to Paper

The first time I put pen to paper
Rumpelstiltskin showed up,
Press clippings in hand of his fairy tale fame,
Had I, he asked, any straw I could spare.
I spoke his odd, cabalistical name,
And he did a jig now all too rare.

The second time I put pen to paper
Cinderella alighted,
Costumed as Eve, gawking Adam, delighted,
Who, thus, unencumbered by ball gown or slipper,
Added spice to her story by precisely revealing
Just where Prince Charming undid her.

The third time I put pen to paper
The Devil arose, aflame his hair,
He discoursed upon his theatrical flair,
The Serpent in Eden, Mephisto in *Faust*,
And, oh, his pride in his portrait hung
In every high class whorehouse

The last time I put pen to paper
Nine Muses complained,
The dead poets wore pains,
But shouldn't the Fates
Bear some of the blame!
Must I alone suffer the shame?

Caring

Circe prone for the man in the moon
But passion's spent where he's marooned
Should I care?

Zeus explains the thunderbolt's use
While Pindar declaims a song of his Muse
Should I care?

His secret discovered, beguiled by Delilah
Samson, shorn, lies helpless in Gaza
Should I care?

Dido, Queen of Carthage, fair
For love of Aeneas, crying her despair
Of course, I care

Aunt Helen

Beyond all fears, Aunt Helen feared
The thunder's pandemonium
Cowering in her craven corner
Petitioning "Dear Lord" to save her
From the rack of the rain's uproar
The whiplash of the zigzag stroke
And what the tempest signified:
The cataclysmic end of days—
From which fears the Lord did spare her,
Though, it seems, from little else.

In the Country of Regret

Traveler, no need to say whence you have come,
But see as far as the eye can see
How only gray sedge dots this barren ground,
How gnarled, bereft, but three trees wait
Though no birds sing in their brown branches.
Dig your heel into this ashen earth,
See how nothing human leaves its imprint here,
How leaden skies hang low above
This creaking frame, its clapboards sprung.
Traveler, Traveler, you should have stopped your ears,
You have closed too late your expectant eyes,
No road leads from this country of regret,
The door stands ajar where you shall dwell.

Labyrinth

The night above moon-rinsed,
I dream a labyrinth,
Its cunning caves crisscrossed,
Wherein you wander lost.

I come to find, from afar,
Your face my only star,
Love's hieroglyph the clue,
The forbidden passage through.

And, by Ariadne's thread
(The Minotaur struck dead),
To bridge the distance true,
From longing unto to you.

A New Dispensation

The gates of the city thrown open,
The citizens festively dressed,
And gathered today in the forum,
To kettledrum, lyre, and lute.
Anxious, expectant their faces,
Excited gestures and talk
(Beyond the usual gossip)
Of a wholly new dispensation.

By special decree of the Council
(Its wisdom applauded by all),
For fear of their swoon at the sight
Of his haughty and garlanded member,
All virgins must blindfolded be,
When aloft on the ramparts the heralds
Triumphantly trumpet the news,
Priapus, our new god, has come.

Hero

Once and then unfallen,
Riding tightrope and dream,
Who, from the stone of circumstance,
Adamant to all the world,
Three times drew forth the peerless blade,
To prove his fey and phoenix life,
And slay the dragon furious.

Errant with visor down,
In kingdoms far from home,
Who, from Circe's amorous bed,
The fierce mendacities of lust,
Woke to spill on wretched fields,
For gracious grail,
His lonely, shipwrecked blood.

Harried by carrion birds,
Crying his fell fate,
That still he must pursue
Drawn to but one face,
Framed by flaxen hair
Her eyes of larkspur blue,
For all his days and ways,
Forbidden to love's gaze

II

In the deep book you read to me,
I a spellbound child,
Wayward in your arms,
Unreconciled to sleep.
Did you know it then.
The story there unfolding
Inexorable denouement,
Beyond all consolation
The future I must live?

Aphrodite

In the Olympian firelight
Reclining upon her couch
Her girdle thrown to the floor
Clad only in her grace
The Goddess unconceals
With a gesture wanton, slow
That terra incognita
Where, all the days of men,
Love and its travails
(The rose, the bed of nails)
Both begin and end

Letter To Aphrodite

Dear Aphrodite

My goddess mighty

With form divine

And smile sublime

I pray you nightly

You to remind

I choose salvation

Of you perilous kind

The Lazarus Problem

The learned are gathered in conclave
(Excluding, of course, Simple Simon)
To ponder the whole thorny question,
The one that for them is so vexing,
Of signs in the sky, ascensions,
And the fuss that, after four days,
He showed up as good as new.
It's the Lazarus problem, perplexing,
Restated with philosophic precision:
How many angels, at his rising,
Could dance with one Pope at Rome?
Tonight, the enigma's performance,
With Herr Dr. Freud in the role
Of the witty deus-ex-machina,
And, in a pro-bono cameo appearance,
The Zeitgeist in his Harvard cap-and-gown.

At Troy

Do you remember,
When Priam, at Troy, was king,
How, at the violet hour,
The palace garden lamp-lit,
You would mount your painted pony,
And with the pipers' song would sing,
As if our world were yet young,
A carousel ride without end,
While I— foreseeing that the Greeks,
With vengeance, were certain to come:
That the Three Crones must have their say—
Whispered as softly as I could,
So that only the gods would hear,
"No matter your hobby-horse journey,
No matter, as if, how far,
Even in the moonlight, you unforgettably bear,
You cannot arrive at our forever somewhere."

Late-Breaking News

Late-breaking news just in tonight from Thrace:

Reporters on the scene have now confirmed,

Beyond the darkest rumors of the town,

The disappearance and, as all clues portend,

The murder of the wood nymph Eurydice

Police have taken into custody,

And charged, as prime suspect in the case,

A local song and dance man, Orpheus,

Whose bizarre claim to mythic lineage.

Son of Apollo and the Muse Calliope,

The Greeks dismiss as but a vain attempt,

By the affianced of the missing girl,

At such defense as insanity affords.

Urged to confess, the culprit only rages

Against "vile Aristeus" and "the viper,"

Feigning strong grief, strumming his lying lyre,

To chant heart-stricken of some deep descent

To Tarturus to rescue his beloved,

And how too soon his glance lost everything,

Not sensing in the street beyond his grieving

The Maenads' frenzied cries of lust and longing—

Their promise to dismember all his songs.

Constantine Cavafy: Poet of Alexandria

Now and again they would gather
In his shabby flat, in the Rue Lepsius,
Upstairs, above the brothel,
Four or five, who, admiring his poems,
Stepped into the candle- and gas-lit dark of his rooms
Always with a certain awe because
This was the scene, as they so often imagined,
Of his midnight struggles to summon
His Lord Apollo's difficult favor,
And, always, they came expecting
(Because he, himself, was of that rare fraternity)
That he would have something new and memorable
To say about those of the Greeks
The most famous in their devotion to the Muse,
Homer and Aeschylus and Pindar, for example,,
But also those, if less celebrated, no less devoted,
Like Callimachus, the Alexandrian,
Poet of the Ptolemies

And sometimes, if he felt that uncanny thing,
The God's favor, had come to him,
So that upon his once blank page,
Beneath his inexplicable pen,
He found lines he recognized as his own,
That spoke to the modern age,
Yet remained faithful to that classical style—
Unadorned, carefully modulated, exact, ironic—
That from the beginning he had taken as his own,
Then, for the sake of those who, in admiration.,
Had come, hoping to savor his latest work,
He felt obliged to put aside his feeling
That what the God had granted him
Should, at least for a time, be kept his alone,
And, so, allowed himself to be persuaded

To recite from the work he had in-progress,
And, because, now, more Helene than Greek,.
Who claimed, for his poetry the whole of the ancient world,
The subject of his poem was as likely to be
The God abandoning Antony at Actium
As Odysseus, for all he suffered
On his long voyage home to Ithaka,
Gaining fabulous riches of experience

But wherever, in his talk, he took them,
However far, through his imagination, they traveled,
The evening was never allowed to end until,
Like Odysseus finding his way home,
The poet, at last, returned to his own Ithaca,
Acknowledging all he owed his time-encrusted town,
The inspiration he drew from its riches of memory and desire,
Knowing that only here, in this one place,
Now more Eve's city, than Alexander's—
This run-down palimpsest of all her equivocal
Incarnations and temptations— could he have
Lived his passions, and become himself,
That only this Muse, only this Alexandria,
Could have given him his poems.

The Macedonian

When, day or night, they accost you in the *agora*,
With their gloomy gossip,
Their conspiratorial lies and rumors,
Do not allow yourself to be taken in by them,
Who are always ready to stir up trouble,
Confiding to you with such irritating assurance,
As if it were news from the Delphic Oracle,
That he only pretends to be one of us,
Because it suits his imperial ambitions,
That, in fact, he has always hated the Greeks,
Who, at Chaeronea, showed his true feelings,
His antipathy to everything that is our pride,
When, without pity (and later
Without the least sign of remorse),
He relentlessly rode down
Rank upon rank of our Theban and Athenian hoplites,
And then, supposing their argument unassailable,
They will defy you to explain
How the incomparable achievements of Hellas,
All the refinements of life in the *polis,*
Can mean anything to him when in his veins
Flows the sinister blood of a barbarian mother.

II

But this is all empty rhetoric and sophistry,
A disaffection which stubbornly refuses to admit
That our destiny is forever intertwined with his,
Whom, at Delphi, the Pythian priestess proclaimed a god.
So, then, when, day or night, they accost you in the *agora*
Stand up to them in their arrogance and dishonesty,
Never allowing them to gloss over
(Because always they find the truth inconvenient)
How, sent by the Macedonian king, Philip, his father,

To study for three years at the Academy,
He came to know what honor is due those immortal names,
From Homer and Aeschylus to Plato and Praxiteles,
Learning, at last, from no less than Aristotle himself
What it means to be one of us,
What it means to be Greek
Nor should you hesitate to challenge
Their mendacious version of recent events
Or their defamations of his character and motives,
Which but parrot the pompous prattle
Of that pretentious windbag Demosthenes.
So explain to them his reasons for crossing the Hellespont,
Marching his incomparable army, first into Phrygia
And, later, beyond the Euphrates, deep into Asia,
Not, as they argue, because of mere ambition,
What would be hubris in an ordinary man,
 But to fulfill the destiny the gods have ordained for him,
The one he, himself, with a stroke, confirmed at Gordium,
But, also, to seek out the Medes and the Persians,
And, never forgetting everything we have suffered
From them, since Marathon, since Thermopylae,
To visit upon them the too-long delayed retribution of the Furies,
And then, you must confront them with the overriding reason
He made the long, dusty march down into Egypt,
To that other shore of our wine-dark sea,
Founding there, in his own name,
What is to be the greatest of all Greek cities,
A capital of memory, preserving to imperishability
Everything Hellas in her glory has achieved,
His great purpose, the one which has driven him all along, being
Not only to conquer the world, but to Hellenize it.

III

And as for those preposterous rumors
Drifting back lately from Persia,
Which are nothing but calumnies
Concocted to discredit him in the eyes of all the Greeks,
Who can believe that at Persepolis,
Where he burned to the ground Xerxes' bejeweled palace,
As sign and seal of Greek hegemony
Over the Persians, who can believe the slander,
That he has begun to wear Persian dress,
And to affect Persian manners and customs;
That he has even taken a Persian wife?

Fairy Godfather*

Forget about it, we had to do it
Because of the ball-breaking shame of it
The way the faggot dishonored the family
So our consigliere gave us the go ahead
But, see, we had to sneak him
You can't just whack a made man
Take down a son of a bitch in his position
You gotta have a serious sitdown
With the *capo di tutti capi*
And the whole metro commission
You gotta get permission
But who's gonna respect us then
If all the other families find out about it
That he had this thing for pansies
Not the kind you bring home to Mamma
On Mother's Day, from the local flower shop
So I asked him, when I whacked him
Whoever heard of a fairy godfather
But I could see he was way too busy to answer
We had to torch his Caddy
Because of all the blood on the back seat

---

* Headline, New York Post, May 1, 2003

Bronstein

(For Woody Allen)

When Bronstein of the St. Petersburg Soviet,
In his arms, to overflowing,
Bouquets of his manifestoes,
Fragrant with the sweat of the proletariat,
Imported not from Paris,
Decadent city of delicate armpits,
But from smoky Pittsburgh and even
Big-shouldered, hog-butchering Chicago,
At last put the finishing touches on
The floor plan of the people's paradise,
The edifice of the Bolshevik future
Rising up gaudily before him,
He could think of only one other moment,
In all of his bourgeoisie past,
As giddily triumphant as this,
That was the day of his coming to manhood,
When, bored to tears by that windbag of a Rabbi,
With his tiresome bar mitzvah jeremiads and admonitions—
"Forget these Hegel and Marx brothers;
Immerse yourself in the wisdom of the Torah"—
He completely outfoxed His Nosiness,
And without help of any kind,
Save the illustrated instructions,
Discreetly posted to him as promised
In a plain, brown wrapper,
Including the inspirational congratulatory letter,
Suitable for framing,
He had, with the abandon of a Cossack,
Initiated himself into
The Royal Order of the Knights of Onan.

On Reading Durrell's *Justine* (1)

Her husband away on business in Cairo,
They drove out to a lonely shore,
To lie, together, in the late day sun,
And there to learn how far they had come,
When, somehow, sensing the urgency,
He opened his eyes to see fixed upon him,
The enigma of her impassioned stare.
Then heard, in never to be forgotten tones,
"It's not just sex, but what, through rapture,
We might arrive at beyond sex."
Words that evoked the recognition in him,
Though one he did not give voice to there,
That they, Justine and all of them, were
Charged particles caught in a field of force,
No longer Alexander's but Eve's city:
That time-encrusted Alexandria
(Love's unfinished palimpsest)
Had become their destiny.

On Reading Durrell's *Justine* (2)

Seven words on her blue paper penned,
He spoke each one he could not comprehend,
That exploded in his mind without pity:
"I bid farewell to love's memorial city."

By day, began to roam her favorite shops,
Imagining their mirrors yet held within,
And. through longing, could be made to yield
Love's image, somehow, once again to him.

And, then, by night, haunting the cabarets,
Where they touched hands beneath a lamp-lit table,
And, in her eyes, saw— he thought—love's truth
Dreamed her actual presence, love's last fable.

Remembering Holly Stevens

Daughter of a famous beauty
And a still more famous poet
You broke your daily bread
In the anxious space between

Wondering why the gaudy heavens
So failed of their conjunction
Neither as luminous as the one
Nor incandescent like the other

But while, silently, you apologize
For failing to win the poet's prize
Shaken, I stare, send thanks to the skies
For what you confide in your smile, your eyes

After

(November 19, 1863)

After the commemorative speaker,
The most celebrated of the Age,
Whom the thousands out of the cities
Made the long journey to hear,
Had, in his two-hour oration,
Honored, with sustained eloquence,
Those who, for the Republic,
On Gettysburg's now hallowed ground,
Were heroes, broken and fallen;
The tall man, gaunt, ungainly,
With fissured face and brow,
Invited as a mere afterthought,
His presence only required
To hurry the day's denouement,
Foreseeing, no doubt, in the press,
The inevitable invidious comparisons,
In ten sentences and less than five minutes,
Spoke his imperishable woe.

Emily Dickinson

Ask,
If you would know,
The unappeasable Fates.
Only they can say,
With their archaic smiles,
Sardonically turned her way,
Where still she holds the lyre,
Still is gowned in white,
Love's anodyne to await—
"She did not choose loneliness,
The loneliness chose her."

Magi

Riding the ridgeline high
Against the moon-lit sky,
With gifts for a king afar,
Wise men, their guide a star—
But come to the stable's door,
Majesty to adore,
Their gaze is lost in wonder:
Not the throne and robes of splendor
Their wisdom had supposed,
But a manger on the floor,
And common swaddling clothes.

Annunciation

As if it were a day like all the others,
She stood with the women of her obscure village,
At the rocky spring on the barren hillside,
Hearing but not listening to their gossip:
The caravan that passed through in the evening
On its way to Caesarea and the sea,
And the Roman legion that, with menacing tramp,
Broke the repose of a quiescent hour—
Tomorrow, she, herself, would be their talk.
Her disappearance the mystery they would ponder.

For fixed forever in her mind's eye,
Holding her spellbound, trembling still,
She saw again, in the Galilean darkness,
That sovereign presence, heard him proclaim once more
The things she knew to be impossible,
To which, nevertheless, she gave her lone assent,
Against the jeering judgments sure to come,
And all the world's weight of profane reason—
That voice, its resonance not of this world, saying.
"Hail, Mary, full of grace, the Lord is with you!"

Paul Arrives in Athens

What is it they have come for,
The refined, the so civilized Athenians?
Is it the truth they seek
Of the robed stranger on the Areopagus,
Wordy with enigmas, or only—
Their curiosity insatiable—
News of the latest novelties,
Whatever is the rage this year
In Antioch and Tyre?
How courteously and attentively they listen
When he speaks of the Unknown God,
But when he mentions the resurrection
Of the dead, those too polite to laugh,
Too urbane to mock him, too Greek
To join the cries of "Charlatan!"
Say only, "Let us hear him tell of this
Some other time," and so depart.
What should keep them—
The Stoics and Skeptics and, especially,
The Epicureans? Her city is theirs,
Athena Parthenos, Virgin Athena,
Voluptuous midnight and stone.
Nevertheless, the Hellenes have heard.
He has disclaimed the old *theia mania,*
Apollo, Dionysus, and the rest of their gods.
The voice of a voice foretelling
Some unknown ardor of this barbarous flesh.

The Other Magus

Or say that the end precedes the beginning,
And the end and the beginning were always there.
                                             T.S. Eliot

Madam, I am the riddling Magus, who has
Studied the thing.

What use to a child this myrrh, whether
Shepherd or king?

As for gold and frankincense, the news is
Their markets are down.

So, with my humble obeisance, this jester
And with him, this clown.

Oh, He'll laugh to see them cavort
On the head of a pin.

And guffaw in His cradle because
They're so bony and thin.

When they opened in Rome, they packed
The old Colosseum.

In Babylon, applauded like sin,
Crowds wild to see them.

Now they polish their act in the streets,
And, pro bono, play mangers.

But, lo, their novel routine
(Oh, the kindness of strangers!):

A once-in-a-lifetime performance,
Prodigious with wit.

And thrills Acrobatic, though with something
Of jugglery in it.

They nail each other to trees,
And pretend they are three

Carpenter, before you go down into Egypt,
Salvage the wood!

Prolegomenon to the Theoretic of Randomness and Whim

Whether ear to ear or merely precise my grin
At the pose of the tabloid Venus, wanton or prim,
I urge, with mute fanfare, your reconciliation to the fact
That the letter in your hands, concise, exact,
The first you have received from the undersigned,
Must be, alas, your final word from him,
Who, annulling the millennial constant of original sin,
The space-time laws of randomness aligns,
Subtracting, from the cosmic lyric, the drag of rhymes,
And veiling the distant dance of the Seraphim.
Meanwhile, I, Herr Exigence von Whim
(The deus-ex-machina, disconsolate, reassigned),
Update the ancient oracles for modern eyes,
To reveal our fated futures randomized.

PS: See how my universal dramatic design
     Plots the false heroic against the mock malign.

IL Miglior Fabbro

(The list of contemporary poets I imagine
speaking these lines is too long to present here)

I am, let us say,
IL Miglior Fabbro, Hooray!
On steep Parnassus I play,
Words, the dragons, I slay,
Oh, the world is but clay
I in beauty array,
On my page lines sashay,
Like sublime Salome,
Nor do truth I betray,
Don't I give sex its day,
Father Freud's and the fey,
The forbidden, the gay—
To the pulpit's dismay?
Let my rivals gainsay
(Though can dross gold assay?)
With rank hubris downplay
What not time can decay.
I the god whom they pray
Where Apollo holds sway,
My crown laurel, theirs hay.

Bugaboo

Solicitously squired through the city zoo,
By my Uncle Frank and his newly intended,
I laugh at the giraffe, with his silly neck extended,
Scowl at the ugliest of creatures, the Gnu,
And applaud the fierce felines, more than storybook true,
But, now, balking at leaving, I, tearfully, complain,
That, somehow, we've missed the famed Bugaboo,
With his pointed horns, and his red suit in flames.

My Father's Photograph

A photograph among your old papers,
You are, it seems, sixteen or seventeen,
In a pose beyond my memory's recall.
For in your arms a violin and bow,
That I never saw, nor ever heard in thrall,
In the time God granted us to be together,
Before the assassin took you from us forever,
But, now, another mystery I must ponder,
Your look is fixed upon a sudden figure,
Who looms before you, whom I cannot see,
Am I wrong to assume I know him too?
Whose nod you await to ordain your playing,
So, in your photograph, what the Muses knew,
That through our broken years, you, too, as I,
Were true to Orpheus whom Apollo made
Lord of the Lyre and all Muse inspired musings,
You with your violin, I with my poems,
Against the frenzied Maenads in their fury.

My Sublime

This, then, the news
From the Garden of Eden
When Adam met Eve
And they found together
The labyrinth of love:
That Men are prose
While Women are poetry
Their difference by
Divine design
But of all those composed
Of meter and rhyme
Yours are the roses
The Poet's prize, thine
You are sublime

My Muse

All through the day, I long for the night
Only then will you come, gowned in the moonlight
With a grace as she of Samothrace
And a smile that lights, sublime, your face
Without your chimes, my rhymes don't ring
It is your songs my poems sing
Loveliest daughter of Memory and Zeus
You are my all, you are my Muse

Homage To Puccini
(In Memory of Giacomo Puccini
Genius of Tenderness)

My Muse whispers, "Play Puccini."
And in awe, oh, how I tremble,
For his music goes all through me
As if I'm Adam, his first morning,
Waking to Eden's great rose dawning.
And, so, inspired, I would sing
For Puccini, rhymes that ring,
Honoring him with Olympian praises,
That would grace poetry's pages,
But how can my prosaic pen
Make lines so lovely, they would chime
With his arias, more than sublime,
And love duets of such tenderness,
We glimpse heaven, though creatures of time.

Puccini and You: A Love Song

(For Doe Lang and in Memory of Her
  Beloved Daughter, Andrea Lang)

There is an old law of love that says
When twilight comes
Night must fall.
So, my Cinderella,
You, my all,
In your glass slippers
Away, you've gone
To some fairytale ball
Where they dance till dawn.
Now I sit in the dark,
Your lovely face to see,
And I play Puccini
My lonely nights through,
Because forever for me,
Only he will do
Whose songs sing you.

In The Poetry of Moonlight
(For Carrie Walker)

Long ago, when I was a young man
I would, as twilight descended around me,
Walk the lamp-lit streets of my city,
Musing upon what made the world go round,
What had been done, and might yet come,
But no matter how long or how far I walked,
One question remained, its answer still hidden,
What passion should rule my days and nights?
What role should I play in the drama of life?
At last, one night, I dreamed destiny's dream:
I walked, at midnight, among moonlit trees,
And a woman, singing, entered the scene,
Gowned only in the moonlight's silver theme,
Like the Nike of Samothrace, she all loveliness seemed,
Then, in the silence, she softly said,
"You must make my music yours alone,
Your words must make my songs your own."
I awoke with a start and a revelation:
In the poetry of moonlight, my Muse had come.

Casandra's Troy

Though neither Greek nor Trojan I am here,
Walking the streets of this legendary city,
Searching the faces in the passing crowds,
For what they expect of their fated future,
Now that Greece's Helen has become Helen of Troy,
Yes, Hector imagines, on some distant day,
On the plain, outside the city's walls,
That he will test his arms, in mortal combat,
Against Achilles and his Myrmidons
To decide, not just his own, but the fate of Troy,
But Hector's is merely a dim presentiment,
Only Casandra, whom no one believes,
Because all assume her lost on the moon of madness,
Foresees what Helen means for the future of Troy,
For Casandra knows the passion that rules the Greeks:
That they, more than any, of all human kind,
Exalt the poetic above all other provinces of mind,
Thus, for the sake of the beauty Greece to Troy has lost,
The Greeks will bear whatever in blood the cost.
So, the Greeks will come, and the walls of Troy will fall.
Then they will sail away with the sublime that is their all.

Hero (The Lost Version)

From the Pantheon of your imagined heroes,
The starry story you would live,
In shining armor, clad for glory,
While high above, love's angel knows,
Though you are small and nearly fallen,
That you wil not come hobbling home,
Until you've slain the dragon Furious,
To make true your pretend play.

Then, you go, with your heroes, riding
(Heroes must hunger, never hate)
Tightrope and dream to demonstrate
Their boyish, phoenix lives because,
Achilles flawed and thunder brave,
They see it all with Merlin's eyes,
But are the vaunted yet the wise?

What did you hope who limped so painfully,
From amorous bed to spill on wretched fields,
For gracious grail, your lonely shipwrecked blood?
Weary of jousts, and beyond the broken years,
Come home at last, memory's gate ajar,
To rooms that tell a keepsake's truth,
Who woke from Circe's arms and art,
From dreams that loomed with shadows of your fate,
To learn—but is it, after all, too late—
Love's compliant heart.

Two-Ton Tony

Enthroned on the raised rear seat
Of an open Chrysler convertible
His beefy arms held victoriously aloft
Or with ponderous clenched fists
Punishing the soft mid-June night air,
Two-Ton Tony Galento,
To a fanfare of honking horns,
Is triumphantly paraded through
The streets of Philly's Little Italy.
Lining the sidewalks, his cheering *paisans*
Caught up in the mummery,
Echo their gladiator's bombastic predictions
Of Roman glory restored, yelling,
"You'll murder the bum, Tony!"
"You'll kill him, Two Ton!"
Before them, in their inspired imaginations,
The sight of the Brown Bomber,
From their hero's brutal blows,
Bloodied and forever broken,
Crashing helplessly to
The Colosseum's canvas.

Meanwhile, the unappeasable Fates above,
Already on to arranging other futures,
Look down upon the antic scene below,
Barely suppressing their sardonic smiles.

Joe Louis knocked out Tony Galento, on a TKO, in the
4th round, June 28, 1939, at Yankee Stadium, after being
floored by Galento in round 3.

Grandmother's House
(In Memory of Pasqualina Rossi)

Is this the house, from here my setting forth?
Iron grate upon the door, your window barred,
The one at which, for more than twenty years,
Ever in black, never forgetting his loss,
Knitting needles flying in your hands,
Or fingering your beads in silent prayer,
You watched Philly's Little Italy parade by.
I know you'd not believe these streets could die,
Here where, with him, you raised nine sons and daughters,
Or imagine the ghostly absences that loom
Before me now in the evening's fading light:
Cola's Apothecary, Bill's Barber Shop,
Carla's Corner Candy, Giovanni's Deli,
And just across Eighth, Froio's Bar and Grill,
Beneath whose glowing neon we would gather—
"DiMaggio's at forty, going strong!"
And "Billy Jazz shipped out today for Pearl."—
Shuttered now against the somber houses.

Remember how (their shiny black Cadillacs lining
Both sides of the block) in custom-tailored suits,
Just like George Raft, *omerta* eloquent
And wiseguys wise, the local Mafiosi—
"Those pansies in the press, they got us wrong;
Some *paisan's* got a problem, we're like the Red Cross."—
Would push their scarfaced way through Froio's doors,
Though not before, looking in your direction,
They tipped, in courtesy, their gray fedoras,
Not hearing you beg Our Lady's intercession.
But with courtesy they could be prodigal,
As the night they wined and dined "Crazy Joe" Garro,
And with the pale spumante, the pretty spumoni,
From the jukebox, in the bar, Sinatra moaning,
They made "*il Pazzo*" an offer he couldn't refuse,

Except, a year or so later, there were rumors
All over the street, how they had Joey measured
For a pair of designer cement shoes, then saw
Him off on an expenses-paid permanent vacation.

On days I had no school I waited with you
For the neighborhood's hoarse-voiced numbers runner,
"Feefee, what's hot?" you'd ask, as if he knew,
Depression dimes weighing down his pockets,
A dumb Tiresias, without a clue.
And then at noon, the radio between us,
Though obscure to me that lovely Tuscan tongue,
I shared with you your imagination's hour,
Because you loved that strangeness, I did, too,
You translating, but mine the epiphany,
Italia opera, I supposed, without the music,
Or perhaps, Francesca da Rimini's tragic story,
Of love foredoomed, that Dante told,
The plot rearranged for radio drama,
He holding her, his questions whispered, urgent,
Who did not sense, as she, stealthy there,
The footfalls of fell fate upon the stairs,
The midnight figures, dire, at the door,
Until the awful knocking, the uproar,
Brought forth his cry of anguish and despair,
"Ma cara mia, che cosa catastrofica?"
Then the heartbreaking strains of your beloved Puccini.

Can I Go Home Again

"Can I go home again," I had asked myself,
Make a final visit of these final years,
Wake in the city I still think of as home,
Walk again the streets of young manhood's dreams?
Taking the dare, and risking I know not what,
With a wave to William Penn atop City Hall,
I head for South Philly, and our old ball field where
With friends, whose faces fill my memory,
I strove in furious games that once had seemed,
More than play, matters of life and death,
To find, not the sward on which we ran and sprawled,
That green oasis amid city cement and stone,
But a gray factory with blacktopped parking lot.
So, I walk the block to the George Washington School
Thinking of ever unsmiling Miss Fitzmaurice,
Severe guardian of the grammar of the tenses,
Expecting to be greeted by the scene
Of children happily clamoring and cavorting
In May Day games around a beribboned pole.
But there is only silence in an empty schoolyard,
And then, I notice the brown window shades,
Like eyelids closed for sleep, are all drawn down,
The wide doors shuttered, seemingly forever
Against the old intrusion of young life.

I drive down Federal to the intersection of Eighth
Realizing, with dismay, as I turn,
That Cola's pharmacy, Froio's Bar and Grill,
And even the Italian grocery are all gone,
Faded "For Rent" signs their forlorn monuments.
I park on Eighth in front of the old three-story
That, after my father's death, we called home,
My mother, my brother, and I, taking refuge there,
With Grandmother Pasqualina, in the family manse,

A house that, ever on Sundays and holidays,
Rang with the voices of her nine sons and daughters,
Who, with their own numerous progeny,
Came to honor her, but also to savor
The ravioli and other Neapolitan delights
She brought forth from the sanctum of her kitchen.

For a moment I consider ringing my old bell
And rousing the usurpers within, who,
Oddly to my sense, now call this home,
Oblivious to the house's human story,
But hesitating, I, at last, wisely, desist—
Wouldn't there be, after all, too much to explain?

I choose instead to walk the neighborhood,
On the chance I'd meet at least one friendly face,
A classmate or a street ball pal of old,
Who, with surprise, would mirror my recognition,
But those I encounter are strangers, everyone,
Their conversations, often, in an alien tongue
As a last resort, I decide to knock on a few doors,
Those once almost as familiar as my own,
But at these, I meet only stares of dark suspicion,
Or hopeless looks of blank perplexity.
Thus, rebuffed, I circle back to my car,
Noticing—unusual in the past—
Several vacant and boarded-up houses,
As well as other once-thriving local shops
That are no longer part of the neighborhood scene,
Replaced, no doubt, by crass discount emporia
In some strip mall inconvenient miles away.

Driving out of the city, deep in thought,
Feeling my journey home has come to naught,
I try to decide exactly what has been lost,
But another question interposes itself,
The one I asked in the innocence of starting out,

And that I cannot escape pondering anew
In the tutelary light of the day's odyssey,
Until, amid the purple dusk descending,
There rises up, before me, the looming figure
Of Heraclitus staring into his river,
Proclaiming the rule of its unceasing current,
That ineluctable law of tide and time
Reverberating, now, in answer, through me,
So that, the truth I've sought is mine, at last,
And I whisper it to myself in revelation,
Knowing I cannot go home again, ever:
"No man can step into the same river twice."

Joey Jazz

I

In your custom-tailored, polished cotton, sky blue
Sartorial splendor, the French cuffs of your maroon
Silk shirt showing just below the sleeves of your jacket,
Expensive black leather shoes, bootblack shined,
A gold chain and cross at your open collar,
Lustrous dark hair, perfectly slicked back,
The tan your swarthy Sicilian forebears bequeathed you,
Features, though more rugged, on the model of the Sheik's,
Hands down, the neighborhood's Valentino,
You put in one of your now cameo appearances
For the benefit of the guys on your old corner.

The wad of bills you flash
(So goes your rumored resume),
You earn as a sort of young exec,
Enforcement Division, South Philly Branch,
Of a nationally influential family-run business,
That especially esteems your powers of persuasion
In those cases, unusual for their recalcitrance,
That do not immediately see the disadvantages
Of turning down the family's magnanimity:
"We made him an offer he couldn't refuse!"

At fifteen, watching you,
This not yet sunset June evening,
The guys on the corner paying you court,
As you are about to head off to Palumbo's
Or one of the local nightspots where
Some hot date breathlessly awaits your coming,
I marvel at your swagger and self-confidence,
And envy you those romantic conquests
I can only, but vividly, imagine.

II

Years later, on one of my visits home,
To see my mother and walk the old neighborhood,
I run into you on Federal, just down from
Your old corner on Eighth. We shake hands,
And—the warmth of your greeting overcoming
More than the estrangement of time—
I learn my mother is not alone
In her pride in her two sons.
But now it is your lament I listen to,
People we knew, events you lived
In those heydays, you nostalgically recall,
Your voice betraying your disbelief
That the way things were will be no more,
While I, forgetting Heraclitus's river,
Look for but fail to find the swagger
That was your signature in your old days.

My criminal defense attorney brother
Keeps me up on what we call
The Philly Follies. So I sense
Where you are headed when you say
(The old *omerta* in abeyance),
"There's been a big imbroglio here here....
Angelo just couldn't see eye-to-eye
With the New York and the North Jersey *paisans*
Over Atlantic City and who is supposed to get what,
Now that Miss America has her high roller boyfriends.
There were some local disagreements, too,
That were not just local, if you know what I mean,
So, the paisans figured out a way
Around the problem of persuading Angie,
And though the snapshot of his last starring
Public appearance made all the tabloids,
It wasn't anything you'd want to keep
For the family photo album,
Or entertain the grandkids with.

So then we had what the headlines
And the stories in the local papers called,
'Mafia Mayhem': Guys disappearing,
Without leaving a forwarding address,
Or turning up, in no condition to complain,
In supermarket dumpsters, or now four-star
Landfills. That finally woke up the D.A.,
And even got the Feds interested,
So some of the guys, maybe the lucky ones,
Have had to change their vacation plans.
Now there are a lot of new arrangements,
And, let's call it, a new commission schedule,

III

This is another not yet sunset June evening,
And you're on your way, not to Palumbo's, but Gino's
For one of his famous Philly cheese-steak sandwiches.
I politely decline your kind invitation to join you.
We shake hands again— this time in farewell,
And I, inevitably drawn to do so, search
Your eyes for that fire that once, unforgettably,
Burned with such intensity in them,
Only to find reflected there, instead,
Despite our differences, that sense
We have strangely come to share,
Of what has been irretrievably lost,
You take a few steps toward Ninth, then—
Because it is important that someone know—
You turn and call back,
"Sugar Ray lost two fights;
I lost only one."

Memoir Published With
"Days Of 1935" in *Italian Americana*

"Days Of 1935" is, I believe, a true piece of Italian Americana, for its focus is my father, Joseph Gabriel, Sr.(originally Giuseppe Gabrieli) whose story was both typical and atypical of the Italian-American immigrant experience. My father (born in 1899) and his sister and three brothers came to America around the time of World War I, from Venafro, a small town, then in the Abruzzo region, settling in South Philadelphia, the city's vibrant Little Italy. When my father reached working age, he did what many of his Italian immigrant brothers did; he went to work in the men's clothing industry. I have no idea what he did in his career as a tailor, though I do remember a large table, in a bedroom of our house, on which were suit patterns, and other implements of the designer's trade. With respect to my poem, however, the tasks my father performed as a tailor are not important. What is important is that, in the Twenties, workers in the men's clothing industry were being recruited into the Amalgamated Clothing Workers of America— the union headed by Sidney Hillman, later a confidant of President Roosevelt—and my father became an ACWA member.

From the many conversations I heard, I judge my father's ideology and politics to have been conservative. Nevertheless, it is clear that, through the Twenties, he became increasingly involved in the affairs of the union, so that, by the time remembered in my poem, the tumultuous and dangerous era of the Great Depression, the union had become a passion and he had become a local official of the ACWA. Thus, the subject of my poem: one of the many informal meetings—in addition to the many formal meetings he was always running off to—my father had, with trusted colleagues, in t6he parlor of our modest row house in Southwest Philadelphia

My poem is, thus, in the first place, about my Italian immigrant father, and what tragically befell him in the era of the Great Depression. The report of my Father's murder, in September 1935, five months after the time of my poem, appeared in the New York and Philadelphia papers. But my poem is also about how my experience of sitting, those nights, in the dark at the top of the stairs and secretly listening to the talk in the parlor below—talk, yes, about union matters, but also about the national and international affairs of the day—profoundly affected my young consciousness and fatefully shaped its future.

W.H. Auden has defined poetry as "memorable speech." The talk I, an impressionable nine-year old, listened to, on such a night as that recounted in my poem, constituted, for me, exactly that: memorable speech. The words, names and expressions I heard, that made so deep an impression upon me, I would recite over and over again, and carefully print in my copybook, as if they were, indeed, a kind of poetry. But if such evenings caused me to begin to care about the sound and sense of words, in the way that poets do, and so served as the genesis of my poetic inclination, that inclination remained essentially dormant through my young years, because I encountered no catalyst that might have stimulated it. Although my education in the academic program at South Philadelphia High School for Boys was excellent, there was relatively little exposure to poetry, other than Shakespeare's plays. Neither in my assigned reading—novels such as those by Dickens, Hardy, Wharton, and Maugham—nor in my own extracurricular reading—Dostoievski, Freud, Jung, Durant's The Story of Philosophy, Nietzsche, and much military history—did I stumble upon the riches of English and American poetry

My life as a poet did not really begin until, with World War II in Europe over—on VE Day, I was on the Elbe River, 45 miles from Berlin—fate or fortune acted favorably on my application to attend the U.S. Army University at Biarritz, France, my first college experience. There, at nineteen, in January 1946, in addition to courses in Logic, Philosophy, and Psychology, I, fortuitously— because he was impressed with my recent reading (Schopenhauer)— was allowed to enroll in Lieutenant Philip Rothman's Literary Masterpieces, an advanced course which began with Dante and concluded with Yeats and T.S. Eliot.

Professor Rothman's reading, at the climax of the course, of Yeats' "Among School Children" and "Sailing To Byzantium" and Eliot's "The Love Song of J. Alfred Prufrock" and "Portrait of a

Lady," struck me like a thunderbolt. I hadn't known such things existed. My gratitude to Philip Rothman is profound. He utterly changed my life. For with his readings of and lectures on modern poetry, the potentiality that had remained dormant within me began, at last, to be actualized. If I have a life as a poet, it really began then and there, which is to say that such a poem as "Days of 1935" ultimately owes its existence to the life-changing experience I underwent at Biarritz, under the influence of Philip Rothman.

Days of 1935
In Memory of My Father

My little brother already quietly dreaming,
I lie in my bed as usual not wanting sleep,
Waiting for what I've learned to wait for,
The locomotive's wail in the great night,
Calling to me forever far down the tracks,
But I listen, now, for what night promised me,
Mother's voice in greeting at our front door,
Then other voices mingling with your voice,
At which I slide from the refuge of my bed
To huddle in secret in the dark at top of the stairs,
As if, I, too, might be— my role obscure—
One of those they call your "*cabaloni.*"

Now, below, your world, in its tangled unfolding,
The tumultuous politics of a dangerous time,
"Roosevelt….the New Deal…. bread lines, still,
A floor on wages, a ceiling on working hours,
The Reds….crisis their game…. then Revolution,
Il Duce and his Black Shirts run Italy now,
The old Italia `e morta….Hitler's rearming,
The world in flames again in five years….".
Words and names I softly say to myself,
That I will keep as if rare talismans,
Printing in my fourth-grade copybook,
And whispering into my pillow like a prayer.

My mother moving now from guest to guest
With fragrant Italian coffee and anisette cakes,
Doesn't know her voice carries up to me,
Listening, to catch every word, in the dark, above:
"The telephone calls have begun again,
The same muffled voice, the same anonymous warnings
Joe dismisses them as empty threats,
As they proved before, but somehow the danger

Seems greater now. I can't help worrying
That this time they won't stop only at threats."
My mother's fears reawaken all of mine,
And I am driven back to the refuge of my bed,
But sleep has become even less possible,
I toss and turn and peer into the darkness
Seeking assurances the darkness never gives,
In the midnight quiet, now, the only sound
Is the locomotive's plaint still calling to me
Through the lonely labyrinths of my memory,
As I begin to know the world as God made it.

Only years later did I come to see
How far you had traveled from that *cittadina,*
Of your own boyhood, in the hills of the Abruzzi,
To those unforgettable nights, when,
Refusing sleep, and with a boy's rapt attention,
I listened to you and your Union brothers
Conspire to make a future you would never know.
Only years later, the truth, at last, mine,
How each step you took to your rendezvous with us,
To those fateful junctures of time and place,
That, in our human blindness, we took for granted,
Brought you only closer to that finality
I know you sensed, but would not evade.

---

cabaloni:: intriguers
`*e morta:* is dead
cittadina: small town

Philadelphia Nights
(In Memory of Russ Baudo)

We walked the cracked mosaic of your city,
Crisscrossed our lives upon its midnight face,
Exchanging news of Rimbaud, praise of Pound,
Rhymed odysseys through streets you grieved unrhymed,
Walnut, Locust, Spruce, Pine, and Lombard,
Down to the Showboat, white jazz for your blues,
Stan Getz, Chet Baker, maybe Terry Gibbs—
And always your wry request: "Ma Rainey's black *Black Bottom.*"
Then making the scene on South, that antic pomp,
Dusky whores shaking their sooty asses
In the crimson neon glow of rundown bars
And seedy-sorry barbecued chicken joints,
You breathing your quiet bravos like a prayer,
As their pimps cruised by in powder-blue Cadillacs.
Then north on Broad and, at the Academy, west
(Ormandy's Brahms still regnant in our ears)
Through Rittenhouse Square, out to the Gilded Cage,
Where the city's bohemia, hunched over cappuccinos,
Forever arriving, like Lenin, at the Finland Station,
Conspired to climb Parnassus from Red Square.
Not you, who raised your cup instead in homage
To pale, passionate Count Axel in his castle
(Your gaze lost there on his too lofty dreaming)
To tell once more his dreaming's deepest cost:
"'As for living…our servants will do that for us.'"

The night we watched Blaze strip on North Eighth Street,
Remember how she plucked her lurid lute,
The undulant slow motion of her truth,
Saint Circe whom all odysseys portend,
Her gyrant grace taunting us to grief.
We left to find two desperate doorways down
A purblind beggar, droll Tiresias,
Who took your dollar for his prophecy:

"Gemlike you burn, sheer incandescence, still
Like any Jesus you'll wear thorny flesh."
"What if" you cried, boarding the streetcar home,
"Obsidian should turn to glaring glass,
This ebon hue succumb to blazing day?"
A tired voice, expended on the moon,
The savage sacrament's voluptuary,
Riding beyond all stops, night's last purlieu

Tristan and Isolde
In Memory of Madeleine Carroll, Actress)

The express hurries you through the mythic evening
To the old city looming at last before you,
The one that in the Delphi of your dreaming
Has summoned you with portents of love's legend,
Though after the downcast years, the dead end days,
The grey-eyed sisters deaf to all your pleas,
You've relinquished all belief in odysseys,
You've come, you are sure, upon a fool's errand.
Still, you hasten through the half-deserted station,
Turn up your collar against the impending chill,
Then step into the actual night you dreamed,
At first unsure, somehow you know the way,
Finding the successive landmarks promised you,
Until you stand before the seventh sign,
The weathered statue of King Mark, Unhorsed,
His saber drawn as if on guard against you,
And here you know you need but turn half way
To see, in blue neon script, against the dark,
The words that, like a runic talisman,
Reveal you've found *Die Opernsangarin*.

All your doubts reemerging now within you
You make your way through the vertiginous night,
To stand before the door heavy with fate.
Inside, a waiting hostess takes your things,
Then, smiling as if, somehow, in recognition,
She ushers you into the room your dreams foretold:
Couples conversing in the glow of candlelight
Their tables in semi-circles around a stage,
Upon which an orchestra waits expectantly,
Shown to the only unoccupied table in the room,
You have barely begun to find your bearings anew,
When—as if a deus-ex-machina had come down
To arrange such a scene as only a god can—

The murmur of voices suddenly dies away
And, with the first breathtaking strains of the *Liebestod*,
You see, upon the stage, miraculously there,
Gowned in the cerulean blue the heavens prefer,
She whom you have always imagined,
She whom you have forever despaired of
Azure-eyed, Seraphically blonde Isolde

Die Opernsangarin: The Opera Singer (feminine)

Hamlet Auditions to Play Hamlet

Clever, Sir, that you heed our casting call
Dressed as the Danish Prince you would play,
In fell melancholy's midnight hue and thrall,
But your doublet's sleeves and collar, how they fray!

And clever, too, your parchment resume,
Wherein you claim as yours this true mosaic,
Complicities of fate and chance that say,
Born at Elsinore, the time archaic,

Gertrude, your mother; Ophelia, more than life,
Stepson to Claudius, your father's brother,
Who stole his crown, and took to bed his wife,
Home from Wittenberg, your tears you smothered.

Conceiving, then, for truth, the play's the thing,
Contrived the troupe to enact with poison vile
Gonzago's murder, to catch with guilt the King,
Your "Mousetrap" baited, rhymed with furious guile.

Though cunning, I concede, Sir, this conceit,
Untutored in our craft, you lack the art
To do the Dane, on or off our street,
Pretend, instead, the clown, as suited to his part.

But if still you would pursue your Hamlet rage,
Be a convert to our method, abandon whim,
Imagine you're the Prince, sublime, off stage,
In all you think and feel, imitate him.

And one thing more, before you're shown the door,
That Elizabethan brogue. you suppose authentic
Is an affectation the critics would deplore,
Since all your speeches would sound cacophonic.

Orpheus Rising

For Viviane Hagner, Fourteen-Year-Old Violin Soloist, In Honor of Her Performance of Saint-Saens' *Introduction and Rondo Capriccioso*, with The Berlin Philharmonic, April 1990.

You make your shyest way past flute and cello
To stand, all fairy godmother gowned in gold,
Stock-still beneath the mute, the poised baton,
Hair raven-black, cut short to helmet's shape,
Pale porcelain faintly rouged at lip and cheek,
Eyes, dark and deep, that know the fabled story—
Stepmother cruel, beauty clothed in rags,
The frantic flight at midnight from the ball—
Can never end with one glass slipper lost.
You are the Cinderella of your Art

And now with dreamy gaze turned far inward,
You raise, in sweet caress, your violin,
As if you held your someday destined lover,
A spellbound prince your playing would transmute,
Deft bow drawn across taut strings,
Nervous vibratos, the wistful swoon and quaver,
A rondo ridden through to sheer caprice,
Until we stare at heartbreak's precipice,
Where, to resurrection, you heed only
The strict, pure, ancient practice of the lyre:

Dismembered Orpheus rises whole again.

Scenario in Red and Black
(After Stendhal)

Two letters, one blood-red, the other black,
Their signatures obscured by her salt tears,
Words as if the engine of the rack,
That sum together all her courage fears:

"Your misalliance heaps upon us shame,
And desecrates through France a noble name."

"To another love I fly in my fashion,
While your drawing room arranges a more suitable passion."

But hers the grand refusal, who will not submit
To contravention of romance's rage,
Who knows, for love, what cost she must remit,
As night must fall, and the Furies mount the stage.

"Let the world revile me, rain down disgrace,
Myself am left at least, and love's unseen face."

Don Juan

Juan, why do you dress once and, then, again,
In sheer redundancy, even when
Your mirror reflects your image with mute alarm?
Think you to double your seducing charm?

Or is it because you fear, at the midnight hour,
Just at the moment when your stratagem
Yields you your prize, you'll lose your horny power,
Leaving, in your lady's bower, no sweet mayhem?

Or perhaps, at last, you've grown too theoretic,
Debating with yourself bedroom decorum,
Which look or gesture, double-entendre so poetic,
Would most persuade love's polemicists in the forum.

One thousand three, in Spain alone, your cult,
Yet, you envy Tristan, true, his lone Iseult.

Elegy for Humpty Dumpty

Humpty, surnamed Dumpty, ovoid man,
Precariously perched on a narrow wall,
By treachery's sly or some inscrutable hand,
Has, upon obdurate earth, grievously fallen,
Alice, the last to see Dumpty intact,
But knew how he tottered, could tumble, be cracked,
Hearing the crash, cried out her alarm
To the king in his castle, fearing Dumpty some harm,
Whence to the rescue rode the architects royal,
Sworn to egg reconstruction and certified loyal,
Who measured and pondered his sprawl to wits' end,
But could not put Dumpty together again.
Oh, for all he endured and how he was blighted,
The king has proclaimed, "Fallen Dumpty is knighted."

Whether mere chance or for reasons profound,
Dumpty was domiciled so far from the ground,
On a wall that afforded him room very little,
So fragile because, egg-like, he was brittle,
And predestined, it seems, to never rebound,
Must be left to those learned in great fall dramatics,
And licensed in the perplex of lapsarian thematics...

Though, in grief, Dumpty leaves no kith or kin,
And the archives record no other like him,
Nor whether, the arrow of Eros in mind,
He pined, on his wall, for an Eve of his kind,
To her infinite absence, fell unresigned,
In nursery rhymes silly, and kids' falldown games,
That tell how he came to looking-glass fame,
Of his station in life, how he never complained,
Nor decried, so confined, the cosmic design—
Divine caprice, or the Fates' fell whim—
We will, Alice sighs, remember and mourn him.

Hunilla

"Hunilla, this lone shipwrecked soul,
out of treachery. invoking trust."

"Norfolk Isle and the Chola Widow"
                              Melville

Padre, Padre, in Payta town this morning,
Before the scrambling urchins raised the dust
Of our mortality through the marketplace
This Corpus Christi, a rapt and rigid rider,
Mounted upon a small, gray ass,
At her slender wrists and where she held the reins,
The dark damask of her skin scathed white,
The salt stigmata of indifferent tides.

And Padre, I saw, too, the sodden shipwreck
Of her gaze, riveted, transfixed,
In spellbound disbelief unwavering,
As though she looked upon a distant dumb show,
From which a coiled basilisk looked back,
And yet her course all wayward and meandering,
As if it were some labyrinth she rode through,
Engraved upon its walls, enciphered woe.

No word or sign of our shared humanity
Did she permit to pass between us there,
At the intricate, slow crisscross of our days,
Nor, Padre, did she yield her errancy,
But journeying still as through a world belittered,
Yet picked her zigzag way among among its ruins,
Nor stopped until beneath *el campanario*,
As if to hear heaven's angelus ring clear.

But the bell that bids us drink the blood-red wine,
And tells whose flesh it is we gulp this day,
Rang not the <u>Ave</u> of our promised bliss,
But making raucous clamor in this ear
Dissonance that fell through desolate air,
As though the Lord of Discord ruled us here,
Drove all upon my tongue the brine she bore,
So that, and on this day, I savored salt.

Elegy For Frances
(In Memory of Frances De Marino)

The book you asked to borrow
Still sits upon my shelf,
You patched its tattered jacket
And rued its rhymes of loss,
Each syllable of sorrow.

But then the news arrived
(The message in the marrow)
That others would survive
The very things you grieved,
The ache of the heart's surmise.

Though I can sum the winters,
Since you turned these pages,
I read your living letter—
"This, only love assuages"—
And I cannot count the cost.

Doris Rose
(Bartlett JHS, Phila.)

Unlike film's famous lovers
Who will always, they know, have Paris
We will have always only
Your smile surprising mine
In the grail of our recognitions
As we passed each other there
On our school's oblivious stairs.
Since then these bankrupt pages
And rhymes that fail of reasons
Fate blames our youthful ages
Our innocence of the heart's true seasons
And then of its contusions,
You smile, and are beautiful, still
I cannot forget you, nor will

Promising
(For Eleanor Greiner Gabriel)

The weather in the castle has turned cold,
And cold the news that tells of majesty
Each day, the grinning Jester at my side,
But dark the great hall, mute the madrigals,
I search the cunning corners of the Keep,
Imagining those talismanic words,
What still the spendthrift years have left unsaid,
Are scrawled in stony silence on these walls.
And then each night, and, yes, forever, too,
The fire low, my candle smoldering,
Upon the scroll the sisters spread before me
(The gray-haired three who spin and count and cut),
Recalling, word for word, first "rose," then "ruin,"
Who at those shabby crossroads we were then,
I rearrange time's dusty bric-a-brac,
And learn anew the wrench of memory.
But now the far horizon closes in,
I hear their tramp, the dark, besieging host,
And feel the final distance of the year,
Dare I trust the sovereign folly of the Fool—
Lies wit beneath that antic guise and whim?
He would I wear his motley, by rote learn,
Imitating his fixed eye and prance,
How to avoid again the backward glance,
The look that lost Orpheus his Eurydice.
Unroll this faded parchment, inch by inch,
And with your finger poised upon the page,
Trace out the cruel chronology of love,
Who at those shabby crossroads I would be,
Done with scarecrow games of let's pretend,
Or wringing from some Dido her salt tears
With what in cindered Troy I say I suffered,
At last unbroken, at last my promise true,
Only, *cara mia,* promising you.

An Old Man Waits For His Alice

Summer's rich profusion nearly done,
I wait at my open door musing upon
The sere, autumnal leaf-strewn days to come,
Then another year's scarecrow finalities.
This is a world, I suppose, as good as any,
But, oh, dear Alice, daughter of my daughter,
You who were all I had, on earth, to love,
I kept you safe through the reign of our afflictions
And shooed the witches from you, the goblins, too,
But what you imagined lured you, at last, away,
Now all I have of you are these fairy-tale letters,
Composed, in your little-girl hand, to friends you said
You'd meet someday through the looking-glass.
Except in that one walk, I could follow you,
But the mirror would not let an old man through,
Mocking me with my helpless reflection there
Until I wearied of that futile stare.
I've thought of the supplications I once knew,
Learned long ago from pious nuns at school,
If only I would keep High Heaven's rule,
But here's the rub— the Times are unbelieving,
And, perhaps, there's naught but what the Fates make true,
Though I am old, I will wait for Alice, grieving.

Lamplighter

At seven or eight, the prospect before me all day,
I would, as evening descended, rose or gray,
Anxiously stand at the railing of our front porch,
And wait for the lamplighter to come with his magical torch,

Searching the distance, in awe, for the sight of him
Finally turning the corner to bless our street.
That the houses held their breath seemed no mere whim,
As I watched him send the darkness into retreat,

Bringing each lamp to life in sudden flame,
Raising his beacons against the reign of night,
Just as, in church, I heard the priest explain,
Over the abyss, God said, "Let there be light."

At last, he came to the lamp just below
Whether ever to return, I did not know,
The faith I kept, he never acknowledged, though,
As I, from above, called softly, "Lord, don't go!"

Story Time

They rub their weary eyes, prop up their pillows
And put off dreaming for a little while,
Wanting something more than they want sleep,
Asking I tell again that age-old story,
"You know, Granddad, the one you liked best,
Your very favorite, favorite, when like us
You were small, and not at all grown up."
I know, of course, which tale they'd have me tell,
A boy of seven, a little girl turned five,
But to draw them out, to hear their wide-eyed version,
Some strangeness they might give to fabled truth,
I feign an old man's lapse of memory,
"Oh, you want the story of the miller's daughter,
And how she guessed the manikin's strange name."
"No? Then the one about rag-clad Cinderella,
And how she wore glass slippers to the ball."

But they are not deterred by my pretense,
"No, Granddad, No! Remember what you said,
When her brothers beg her not to leave them ever,
And the Beast so misses her he nearly dies,
That seemed so much a mystery to us then,
We asked you, please, to say it twice again."
And now in awe I hear their exact recall
Of an old man's fond and moonstruck maundering,
Musing I'd not intended for them at all,
Or only someday when in ivied halls,
Reading themselves to sleep in some great book,
They'd puzzle through anew to paradox,
As they learned it long ago in love's story,
The truth that, in our midnight cogitations,
And even in the light of lucid days,
Perplexes us with its Janus face
(As she, the Nike, gowned in marble grace)—
"Beauty so beautiful her beauty hurts."

So What's It Like
(In Memory of Jeanne Crain, Actress)

They had talked, through the evening, about nearly everything:
Their childhood bedtime stories, nighttime fears,
The din of college, the frustrations of their careers,
And the cries with which the obscure future might ring

Then, in the summer night, just at her door,
The films Hollywood doesn't make anymore,
Those romantic comedies that told how the sexes rhyme,
Their charm enough—"We have the classics for the sublime."

Romance, thereby, at last, for them, the theme,
"So what's it like?" she wistfully asked of him,
Love, she meant, he knew—no mere whim,
But the misty–eyed memory of another scene.

He might have responded with love's ancient news:
"It's the thing all of Midas's money couldn't buy,"
Or, a quotation from *Bartlett's* of more modern use,
But he knew they wouldn't do for her heart's cry.

So, he took her in his arms, and risked the dare,
To show her what words could not—
How much he found her fair.

Law of Love
(On an Observation In Durrell's *Alexandria Quartet*

They walk by each other in a city street,
That common thoroughfare, for him, transfigured
The moment he catches sight of her lovely face,
Yet no sign of recognition passes between them,
No fleeting smile, no simple wave of the hand,
Only, those bittersweet moments, gone too soon
Ladylike, she must keep, he knows, to convention,
What's more, upon the one approaching there,
She sees the signs that tell the toll of time
While he, in turn, is bound by Nature's rule,
That forbids those yeas from intruding upon young grace.
Futile, then, the protest he might raise,
For the Fates must have their sardonic say,
And the Law of Love is a game we are made to play:
Somewhere, in life, we shall meet the right one,
But always, alas, at the wrong time.

Agent 007

He read the promise in her telegram:
Venezia, her city, she— beguiling,
To dream adrift with her in gondolas.
So took the midnight flyer south, from Paris,
Schooled in deceit, a master of disguises.
But now, with covert glance, he recognizes
Beneath the broad-brimmed hat, pulled low to hide them,
The cold, gray eyes. "Beware," the cypher warned,
"The cane on which he leans to feign his limp."
Let quibbling casuists complain
That scruples are to him but mere convention,
Or yet a stale theatrical contrivance
Intended to delay the denouement.
Through his coat he slyly pats his Walther—
Purblind who think chess the great game.

Days of Junior High and War

(For Debra Caswell)

Not yet men who make their way to school,
On spring's most lucid morning, far from
The deep caresses of their distracted mothers,
Upon the street's despair, run roughshod
Till the bell rings; then—pledging
Their grim allegiance—watch with
Wandering attention, as the teacher,
His pointer upon a red-lined battle map,
Tells the new, but ancient, news of war.
Windows are opened on ordinary places,
Matthew, Mark, and John— for whom winter
And the war are as far away as anything—
Scribbling their fierce and final ultimatums,
Bring to crisis their rivalry over Helen,
For them, the fairest girl in all the school.
Meanwhile, as the teacher tries to quell the turmoil,
Dim perceptions push their human fingers
Across the shadowed face of Joseph, who,
Sitting last in the third row of the creaking world,
Though sharing the admiration for the lovely Helen,
Is preoccupied with what the battle map foretells:
That, again, the walls of Troy are doomed to fall,
And other legions will conquer Caesar's Gaul.

Remembering Ingrid Bergman
(What I Might Have Said)

A blond Valkyrie amid our khaki crowd,
Almost as shy as you were beautiful,
You took refuge at the only unoccupied table,
Though soon surrounded by GIs in awe.

You had come with the famous radio comedian,
And half a dozen stars of stage and screen,
To help us dull the still insistent memory
Of Normandy's bloody tides and the Bitter Woods.

That was five years before, with your Italian director
(The tabloid headlines all but screaming, "Whore!")
You scandalized, for love, two continents.
And how many years since then until I knew,
Ransacking ancient wisdom, the poem's lore,
What I might have said had we spoken.

Love Letter

Not knowing where on earth this night you are,
What street address to mail this letter to,
Whether there are memories we yet share, like a star,
Still, I send, sincerely, love's news, at last, to you.

Nor knowing, then, how poets sing their praise,
Your books under arm, I'd walk you home from school,
Not out of chivalry, or some golden rule,
But for the beguiling grace in all your ways.

You moved away, while I went off to war,
The dice were thrown; I saw your face no more,
I don't know why I let the years slip away,
Allowed those dice to have their capricious say.

Only, that the young are prodigal, let life be fate,
Recognition comes with age, so comes too late.

Delores: Love's Story

Our fathers were old country <u>paisans,</u>
And we, new playmates for a winter's evening,
I recall straight light brown hair,
And features of such porcelain delicacy,
That, through the veil of years, astonish still.
You took my hand and kindly led me to
A lamp-lit loveseat where, side-by-side,
We sat in warm and shy intimacy,
Then, half in apology, you explained
(I would worry much about it ever after,
And see what made you wise beyond your years),
"Each week, the doctor comes, with his black bag,
To listen to the beating of my heart."

Then, still with earnestness, but sweetness, too,
You said, "I thought all day about your coming,
What we might do, together, our first evening,
So, here, for us, is my _Blue Fairy Book,_
I'd like to read, to you, my very favorite,
It is, I know, a fairy tale love story,
And boys prefer more adventurous tales,
But should you come to care for it as I do,
And share with me why I love it so,
Then more than just playmates for an evening,
That would make us special friends forever."
And so you read "BeautyAnd The Beast,"
Leaving me, in my perplexity,to ponder
What you could mean by your enigmatic,
"More than a love story, it's love's story."

It is now more than a half -century since
Our *Blue Fairy Book* evening together,
My father died, our families grew apart,
Never again would I hear you tell love's story,
Now, I cannot forgive myself for allowing
Life's hurly-burly to obscure and lose you,
Forsaking you, I fear, to no fairytale future,
Those doctors, listening to your beating heart,
Did they know how rare the life they held
In the learned fumbling of their hands?

This is a winter's night like long ago,
Your fragile form palpable in the lamplight,
As I take up once more the gift you gave me,
To read, again, in my *Blue Fairy Book*
Your beloved "Beauty And The Beast,"
Imagining that still I hear you saying,
What, precociously, you knew in your young years,
The enigma you sweetly left me to ponder—
"More than a love story, it's love's story"—
That, belatedly, I've come to comprehend,
(Too late to make the difference it should have):
It's Beauty's love that transforms the Beast
Into the handsome Prince of all her dreams,
So, mine, your bequeathed epiphany,
The truth you knew of love's poeticizing power,
That *caritas* can transfigure the gargoyle world,
Transmute the beastly into the beautiful,
You, my pale muse of tenderness,
Whose hold on life was only gossamer.

Delores: Love's Story
(Addendum)

Midnight and I rose to go,
But how could I bear farewell to thee?
As you held out pale hands to me
And, smiling sweetly, softly said,
"There are more tales that want to be read."
But despite the message of your smile,
I saw tears fall from your eyes,
That puzzled me in my young days,
Until I trod life's gray byways---
Those doctors, with their black bags, who
Came to mend the murmurs of your heart,
Loomed like shadows ever over you,
Without avail, their arcane art:
You never knew, when "Goodnight," your cry,
Would be, forever, your own, "Goodbye."

You Who Never Arrived
(After Rilke)

Wasn't that you I glimpsed in the Mardi Gras madness?
Didn't you hear my cry through the carnival din?
Round and round, whirled in the carousel's orbit,
You stroked his golden mane and whispered sweetly
Your aria to the calliope's mechanical song,
To calm your pretty pony, reassure him,
Such care, I thought— the kiss of *caritas*—
Unmasked your masquerade, told who you are,
But the hurly-burly turned to valediction,
And the vertiginous night revealed your vanishing.

Wasn't that you I saw at the Gare du Nord?
In the purple dusk that everywhere descended around us,
As if a great longing had caused a curtain to fall,
And from only offstage could be heard the actors' last lines,
So that, as I looked out through love's anxious window,
The one I composed for you on every journey,
I recognized, in a compartment opposite mine,
One of us arriving, the other departing again—
The distance between us, an enigma without a solution—
You whom I have, always, imagined.

Wasn't that you that night at the Musikverein?
The Vienna's all Tchaikovsky program sublime,
With my opera glasses, I, suddenly, found you there
In a box on the other side of the Golden Hall,
Stunningly gowned in violet, Isolde fair,
Your breathtaking presence holding me in such thrall,
I imagined the *Da Rimini* being played just for us,
Then, I scrambled through the crowd, desperate to find you,
Begging the Fates to permit our paths to cross,
But I found, only, a cold moon turned blue,
You, I sought, again, in the night I lost

Wasn't that you I might finally have found,
But for a day, at the Hotel Tristesse?
You, as this blurred photograph shows,
 Standing before an astonished pier glass,
Its luminous surface holding you there,
Refusing to relinquish your shimmering form,
While, under the lamp-lit spell of evening
You, with your soft hands, arranged
The white gown you will trail forever
In the dust of my desolation—
You who, loved from the start, never arrived.

Odyssey

When you come to the burden of your fate,
To that imperious thing inside you
Straining all your sinews,
Do not examine it too closely,
Do not delay,
But remembering Orpheus
And the admonition against looking back,
Step forthrightly into the path
The Three Sisters have marked out for you,
You will not be long in coming to your own
Scylla and Charybdis, your own lustful Circe,
Though yours is not the journey royal Odysseus made,
The one that, at last, turns round upon itself
Toward Ithaka, faithful Penelope, and home.

Not for Menelaus, then, your delirium at Troy,
Nor for Agamemnon and the honor of the Argive cause,
Nor even for Hellas, though her glory is your pride,
But always for Helen, only for her,
Choosing over and over again,
Alone in the starlit Ionian night,
The same gorgeous fatality
That Paris chose but once,
And when Babylon's crooked streets entice you,
As they surely will,
As all the oracles have foretold,
Remember this in your passion,
Those streets you have entered,
With their houses of desperation—
Their lamp-lit doors ajar,
The Sirens crying your name,
With promises for a god—
They are not what you imagined,
They are not love's labyrinth.

Farther than far Samarkand is your journey,
But do not waver in your allegiance,
In your obedience to what lies deep within you:
Your devotion, above all, to the service of the Muse,
And though the road you travel
Has been forsaken by the Gods
Though always, for you, a crisis of arrival,
Always the desolation of departure,
There is for you this solace

That sometimes during the reign of night,
You wake to see, shimmering before you,
The loveliness you have, always, imagined,
The sublime Helen of your dreams,
And though, with your realization
That she is only an apparition,
She disappears into the midnight of your sorrow,
Still, you take her appearance as a portent
Of what, in the distance, lies before you,
So, never faltering in your purpose
Undeterred, despite even this,
That incomparable beauty doomed a city,
And, in the end, counting yourself fortunate,
Fortunate in the fate you have been granted,
The fate you have forever chosen,
An odyssey with an Ithaca of your own,
An odyssey with the Helen you long for.

Biographical Note

Joseph Gabriel (his birth certificate says Joseph Gabrieli) was born April 13, 1926, the son of Almarinda Rossi Gabriel and Joseph Gabriel Sr. (originally Giuseppe Gabrieli). He grew up in South Philadelphia, the city's vibrant Little Italy, attending public schools there, and graduating, from South Philadelphia High School for Boys, in January, 1944. With World War II on, not waiting to be drafted, he enlisted in the U.S. Army and was sent to Fort Bragg, NC, for Basic Training in Artillery Fire Direction Control, the placement officer deciding he possessed the necessary mathematical aptitude. Eventually, he was sent to Europe, serving in the S2 (Intelligence) section, of the 34th Field Artillery Brigade Headquarters. When the war in Europe ended, his unit was on the Elbe River, 45 miles from Berlin. While in the Army of Occupation in Germany, he had the opportunity to attend the U.S. Army University at Biarritz, France, for the semester beginning in January, 1946, taking courses in philosophy, psychology, and literature. In "Masterpieces of Western Literature," he was introduced, by LT. Philip Rothman, to modern poetry (Yeats and T.S. Eliot)—an experience that proved a revelation and that changed his life. Later that year, after his discharge from the military, he matriculated at Villanova University, majoring in philosophy and English, and graduating, in 1950, first in his class. After Villanova, he undertook MA and PhD studies in English at the University of Pennsylvania and then went on to teach at LaSalle, Drexel, Central Michigan University, and Central Connecticut State University, specializing in American Literature. Of all the courses he taught, his favorites were two that he originated: "The Problem of Evil in Hawthorne, Melville, and Henry James" (the subject of his interminable, never submitted PhD..thesis) and "Twentieth-Century Thought and Literature," which combined his interests in the thinkers who created the Twentieth-Century intellectual climate (Marx, Lenin,, Bergson, Einstein, Freud, Jung, Sartre, Dewey, Spengler, Toynbee, Whitehead. etc.) and the writers who created the literature that belongs to that intellectual environment (Proust, Mann, Joyce,

Gide, Kafka, Koestler, Pirandello, O'Neill, T.S. Eliot, Hemingway, Fitzgerald, Camus, Durrell, etc.). Of course, each time "Twentieth-Century Thought and Literature" was given, representative works from only 6 or so such writers could be accommodated. He was married to Eleanor Greiner Gabriel, by whom he has two sons, Kevin Knute and Terence Joseph.

Poetic Credo

Contemporary poetry is dominated by an adherence to the poetics of Indeterminacy, in which tuneless chaos prevails over music and meaning. In their determination to subvert the traditional conventions of poetry, contemporary poets dismiss, in their practice, all the time-honored devices that make poetry poetry, such as, for example, rhythm and rhyme, symbol and song. That is to say, they dismiss Auden's famous formulation that poetry is "memorable speech"—a unique and compelling combination of sound and sense.

Rather than joining my peers in their nihilistic revels, my intention, on the contrary, is to employ the traditional practices of poetry to achieve Auden's ideal. Taking that ideal as my own; that is, taking the practice of such great modernists as Dickinson, Robinson, Yeats, Rilke, Pound, Eliot, Cavafy, Stevens, Hart Crane, and Auden, I seek—against the indeterminacy that defines contemporary poetic practice—to make poems memorable for their music and meaning, their sound and sense.

Thus, whether attempting a lyrical love poem or a poignant memoir of my growing up in Philly's Little Italy, my intention is to create a dramatic poetry that is to be spoken as well as read, heard as well as seen. Therefore, my poetry stands as a direct challenge to the nihilistic conception of poetry that rules the contemporary literary landscape.

CPSIA information can be obtained
at www.ICGtesting.com
Printed in the USA
LVHW012053150419
614197LV00010B/335/P